HORSES SET I

PINTO HORSES

BreAnn Rumsch

ABDO Publishing Company

visit us at
www.abdopublishing.com

Printed in the United States of America, North Mankato, Minnesota.
042010
092010

 PRINTED ON RECYCLED PAPER

Cover Photo: iStockphoto
Interior Photos: Alamy pp. 11, 15, 19; Corbis p. 12; iStockphoto pp. 13, 17;
    Peter Arnold pp. 5, 9; Photolibrary pp. 7, 21

Editor: Heidi M.D. Elston
Art Direction & Cover Design: Neil Klinepier

Library of Congress Cataloging-in-Publication Data

Rumsch, BreAnn, 1981-
  Pinto horses / BreAnn Rumsch.
      p. cm. -- (Horses)
  Includes index.
  ISBN 978-1-61613-421-1
  1. Pinto horse--Juvenile literature. I. Title.
  SF293.P5R86 2011
  636.1'3--dc22
                                                    2010009931

CONTENTS

WHERE PINTOS CAME FROM

Horses have captured the imaginations of humans for hundreds of years. They make beautiful companions for work or play.

Horses have been around for about 60 million years. Their earliest ancestor was a fox-sized creature called eohippus. Today, many different **breeds** and colors of horses exist. These powerful mammals belong to the family **Equidae**.

Spanish explorers brought pinto horses to North America in the 1500s. Eventually, pintos became an important part of American life. Farmers, ranchers, and travelers put them to work.

In 1947, U.S. pinto enthusiasts started the Pinto Horse Association of America (PHAA). Today, pinto horses are a popular choice for competitors as well as pleasure riders.

Pinto *is the* **Spanish word** *for "painted."*

WHAT PINTOS LOOK LIKE

Pintos are not a true horse **breed**. Instead, they are a color type. A color type horse is bred for its color or pattern. The color type may be displayed in many different breeds.

A pinto horse's shape and other body features depend on its breed. With so many breeds, pintos come in four sizes. They are miniature, miniature B, pony, and horse.

Horses are measured from the ground up to their **withers**. At 34 inches (86 cm) or fewer, miniature pintos are the smallest. Miniature B pintos stand up to 38 inches (97 cm) tall. Pinto

Pintos are known for their bold, colorful coats.

ponies measure between 38 and 56 inches (142 cm) tall. Most ponies weigh less than 800 pounds (360 kg).

The largest pinto size is the horse. These animals stand at least 14 hands high. Each hand equals four inches (10 cm). Most pinto horses weigh up to 1,300 pounds (590 kg).

WHAT MAKES PINTOS SPECIAL

Before the Spanish brought horses to America, Native Americans had never seen these animals. But soon, Native Americans favored pinto horses for their coloring. The horses were easy to camouflage with tribal paint.

Cowboys also valued these horses. Pintos could handle hard work and the rugged land of the West. In addition, every pinto coat was **unique**. The cowboys used the distinct coloring to identify individual horses.

Today, the PHAA registers 19 different horse **breeds** as pintos. Registered pintos are commonly quarter horses, Thoroughbreds, or Arabian horses. Other **breeds** include Morgans, American saddlebreds, and Tennessee walking horses.

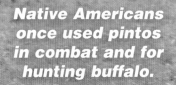

Native Americans once used pintos in combat and for hunting buffalo.

COLOR

The two recognized color combinations for pinto horses are piebald and skewbald. A black-and-white pinto displays the piebald coloring. A pinto with skewbald coloring is white with any color except black.

Overo and tobiano are the two color patterns for pintos. An overo pinto has a colored coat with white patches. The patches have jagged edges.

An overo's white spots never cross its back. This horse has a dark tail, mane, legs, and back. An overo commonly has a **bald face** marking on its head.

A tobiano pinto is a white horse with colored patches. The patches have smooth edges and may cross the horse's back.

A tobiano can have a two-tone mane and tail. All four legs are usually white below the knees and the **hocks**. Tobiano head markings include a star, a stripe, a **snip**, and a **blaze**. If a tobiano has a **bald face** marking, the horse is usually called a tovero.

No two pinto coats are exactly alike.

CARE

Horses need special care from their owners. A pinto horse kept in a stable should have its own

Each tool in a grooming kit has its own purpose.

stall. Plenty of clean bedding and fresh air will help keep your pinto comfortable.

A veterinarian should examine your pinto at least once per year. He or she can provide **vaccines** and **deworm** the horse. The veterinarian can also file down any uneven teeth. This process is called floating. It can help avoid mouth injuries and chewing problems.

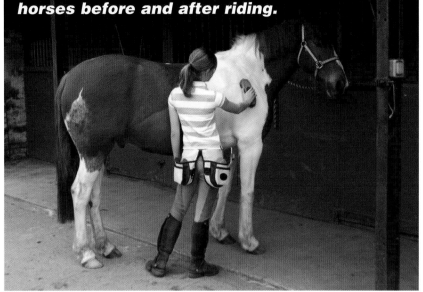

Your pinto horse also needs to see a farrier every six to eight weeks. He or she can trim the horse's hooves and replace its horseshoes.

On a daily basis, you should clean your horse's hooves with a hoof pick. This prevents dirt and stones from getting stuck and causing pain.

Hoof care is just one part of daily grooming. Grooming your pinto's coat will also keep the horse happy and healthy. A rubber currycomb and a body brush are useful for removing dirt. A grooming cloth adds shine to the clean coat.

FEEDING

In the wild, the horse's natural food is grass. Stabled horses eat hay, which includes dried grasses and alfalfa. Hay makes up the largest portion of a pinto horse's diet. It can be fed in a hay net hung in the horse's stall.

Stabled horses also eat grains. Common types include barley, corn, and oats. Oats are a favorite of pintos!

Your pinto needs to eat about three times each day. The amount an owner feeds his or her pinto depends on how active the horse is. Fresh, clean water should always be available.

Many owners also give their horses **supplements** such as salt and cod-liver oil. These substances provide the horses with important vitamins and minerals.

Horses naturally lower their heads to eat. They will eat oats and other grains from a bucket on the ground.

THINGS PINTOS NEED

Pintos are great horses for riding. To enjoy the best possible ride, owners need proper tack. Tack includes saddles, saddle blankets, stirrups, and bridles.

A saddle offers a rider a smooth ride. It also spreads the rider's weight over the horse's back. Riders can choose between Western saddles and English saddles. Ranchers and trail riders use Western saddles. English saddles are more suitable for racing and jumping.

A rider places a saddle blanket under the saddle. This pad absorbs the horse's sweat and prevents the saddle from slipping. Stirrups hang down from either side of the saddle. They support the rider's feet.

The rider uses a bridle to control the horse. The bridle fits on the horse's head. It attaches to a bit, which fits in the horse's mouth. The rider holds on to reins that attach to the bit.

Tack should fit a horse well to prevent pain or injury.

How Pintos Grow

A horse's mother is called a mare. The male parent is a stallion. After mating, a mare may become **pregnant**. She carries her young for about 11 months. Then, she gives birth to a single baby horse. Sometimes, a mare may have twins!

A baby pinto horse is called a foal. The pinto's first hours of life are full of new discoveries. It will learn to stand within the first hour. Within another hour, it will begin to drink its mother's milk. The mare nurses her foal for about six months.

The pinto foal is born without teeth. As it grows older, it grows milk teeth. These are replaced with permanent teeth by age four or five.

Baby pintos are able to run just a few hours after birth!

After the foal is **weaned**, it joins other young horses. They sleep, eat, and play together. These activities help the young horses grow strong and healthy. Most horses live 20 to 30 years.

Training

Training a horse requires patience and skill. Horses learn lessons one at a time. A trainer works with a horse slowly. He or she repeats certain sounds and movements. Eventually, the horse connects these sounds and movements to desired actions.

Like all horses, a pinto learns most easily at a young age. One of the first lessons an owner must teach a pinto is how to wear a halter. This piece of tack fits over the foal's head like a collar. Soon after, the foal learns to lead on a rope. Leading is similar to how a dog walks on a leash.

Pinto horses should not be ridden until they are at least two years old. Until that time, their bones are still growing. A human's weight could easily injure them.

Before riding occurs, a horse must be comfortable wearing a saddle. Once a pinto can safely be ridden, it can train for many different sports and jobs. With proper training, these colorful horses make great companions for any horse lover!

A horse learns every time it is with a human.

GLOSSARY

bald face - a white, wide marking covering most of an animal's face.

blaze - a usually white, broad stripe down the center of an animal's face.

breed - a group of animals sharing the same ancestors and appearance. A breeder is a person who raises animals. Raising animals is often called breeding them.

deworm - to rid of worms.

Equidae (EEK-wuh-dee) - the scientific name for the family of mammals that includes horses, zebras, and donkeys.

hock - a joint in a hind leg of a four-legged animal. A hock is similar to a knee joint, except that it bends backward.

pregnant - having one or more babies growing within the body.

snip - a white marking between a horse's nostrils.

supplement - something added to make up for a shortage of substances necessary to health.

unique - being the only one of its kind.

vaccine (vak-SEEN) - a shot given to prevent illness or disease.

wean - to accustom an animal to eating food other than its mother's milk.

withers - the highest part of a horse's or other animal's back.

WEB SITES

To learn more about pinto horses, visit ABDO Publishing Company on the World Wide Web at **www.abdopublishing.com**. Web sites about pintos are featured on our Book Links page. These links are routinely monitored and updated to provide the most current information available.

INDEX